TIME OUT

A collection
of kickstart
prayers for
teenagers

DAVID GATWARD

kevin
mayhew

First published in 2002 by
KEVIN MAYHEW LTD
Buxhall, Stowmarket, Suffolk, IP14 3BW
E-mail: info@kevinmayhewltd.com

The prayers originally appeared in *Get Real, God!*
and *Get Real, God! 2.*

9 8 7 6 5 4 3 2 1 0

ISBN 1 84003 951 5
Catalogue No. 1500533

Cover design by Jonathan Stroulger
Edited and typeset by Elisabeth Bates
Printed and bound in Great Britain

Contents

For Nina –
thank you.

Foreword

Excuses, excuses, excuses. We've all got them and we all use them. Especially when it comes to prayer. But think about it, have you ever heard of a friendship which survived with no communication, no talking, no getting to know each other better? No. Exactly. So why do we make excuses about prayer when getting to know our creator is fairly important? Well, everyone has their reasons, but all that's important is that excuses are just that – excuses, not solutions.

This book, though, is not a solution. It's not going to erase your excuses or give you instant communication with God. What it is, though, is something to help you take a bit of time out for a creator-chat.

This is not a book to be read from start to finish. This is not a book full of twee answers and ideas to reinforce things you feel comfortable with. What it is is a collection of ideas, thoughts, questions, challenges and prayers, to give you a kickstart if you ever need one. And if you're anything like me, that's every day.

Keep it by your bed, spill coffee on it, write on it, forget about it and then find it years later. . . . Whatever you end up doing with this book, always remember that if you find excuses getting in the way all you need to do is stop, take some time out, and say a prayer. It's not difficult, it doesn't require you to learn the Bible from cover to cover and then speak in tongues. All it actually requires is honesty, an open mind, a willingness to learn and a little bit of time. So open a bag of crisps, crack open a can of your favourite fizz and, while you're at it, see if you can find that Bible of yours . . .

DAVID GATWARD

Creation

Do

Cook something, right now. Get into the kitchen and make something amazing, something tasty. Isn't creating something the best feeling in the world?

Think

You've got relationships with friends and family. How is it that these relationships work? Is it all down to one person telling the other what to do, or is there a sense of freedom? Is there a hint of risk in relationships for them to work? Why do you think this is? What would a relationship be like if there was no freedom, no risk?

Pray

Lord, it's always bothered me
    (well, not *always*; you know what I'm like)
    that in this world
    that you created
    you *allow* evil to exist.

Now I've heard all the arguments
    (unless, of course, the sermon sent me to sleep)
    and they all make sense.
This business about you
    wanting a 'relationship' (scary word, Lord)
    with us.

I know a relationship
    needs freedom on both sides.
I know that it requires a degree of risk
    (especially with me)
    but does it really require the risk
    that seems to cause
    all the bad in this world?

It doesn't make sense, Lord.

I'm not asking for any visions,
    or God-like voices to wake me in the night
    and explain this.
I just wanted to tell you how I felt.

Which in itself is part of the risk
    of the relationship we share,
    isn't it?

Thanks for listening, Lord.

Amen.

The real you

Do

Find a mirror, anything that'll show your reflection. Grab it, look at it, look at you. What do you see? Just a person? Just a face, a few spots, hair that needs washing? Or do you see more? A person with dreams and hopes and fears and failings and potential?

Think

There's more to you than just a reflection. There's more to you than those bits you don't like. It's about seeing beyond the reflection and getting to the real person. When you look in the mirror you find it hard to like what you see. Do you think God sees just this or looks further, looks beyond the reflection and sees more? God sees the bad in us all but concentrates on the good. What good, what potential stares back at you from the mirror?

Pray

I don't like me, Lord.
I really don't.

I'd consider myself a very good judge of character
    (I talk to you, after all)
    and I know why I like other people
    or why I don't,
    and I know why I don't like me.

I see me from the inside,
  and it's a bit of a mess in here.

I'm sure there are bits even you can't see
  because if you knew
  what I knew
  you wouldn't like me.

I sound a bit melodramatic, don't I?
I can't help it;
  it's just that at the moment
  when so much is going on
  in my life
  I can't help but look in the mirror
  and wish it was someone else's reflection.

Lord,
  it's extremely difficult
  to be totally convinced
  that out of the dung heap that I see myself as
  flowers will grow.

Help me through the winters, Lord,
  so that I'll see the summer.

Amen.

Stubborn

Do

Got something you think you're utterly convinced about? Ever been in one of those situations where no matter what someone else says, you still think you're right? Perhaps you should revisit exactly what that issue was and take another look. No one's saying you're wrong, but there's a chance you're probably not entirely right either.

Think

Life is all about learning. Every breath of every day we learn something new – good, bad, exciting, frightening. To learn, we have to be open, willing to listen, to understand others, their views, ideas, thoughts, aims, problems.

Pray

I'm stubborn, Lord.
Are you?

I don't mean to be so abrupt,
    but sometimes I just need to be.

So, Lord, are you?
Do you sit there all huffy
    until everyone believes the same as you?

I guess you're in a unique position though.
You *are* right.
(I think.)

You see, Lord,
    when I think I'm right
    I can be very stubborn.
After all, why should I change
    just to fit in with someone else?

But, by the same token,
    why should they change
    just to fit in with me?

And then you have loggerheads.

Lord,
    teach me to change direction a little more,
    learn how to slow down,
    and give way.

I don't want
    to keep on crashing.

Amen.

An exciting life

Do

Grab nearest Bible and read 1 Kings 17:1-6. OK, so perhaps doing what Elijah did isn't exactly your idea of fun. But, just for a minute, try to imagine the life he led. No nine to five, no need to buy the next best thing. It was a life on the edge and occasionally on the run as well.

Think

What kind of life are you aiming for? What are other people trying to convince you is important? Who are you listening to? What are your real dreams for your life? How are you going to achieve them? Where does God fit into all this? What are God's dreams for you?

Pray

Elijah was mad, wasn't he?
Well, he must have been.
Doing what he did
    and having to be fed by crows
    just to stay alive.

Lord, could you give me a little
    of that madness?

I know it's a strange request
    but I look around at so many people
    and their lives seem so . . . dull.

There is no risk, no adventure
   no excitement.

Elijah knew what these were really like, Lord.
I admit that he may have taken things a little far
   (but don't try and convince me it was *his* idea),
   but at least he knew excitement.

And he did it for you.

I don't know what kind of
   modern day equivalent there is
   (bungee-jumping for Jesus?
   cave-diving for Christ?)
   but there must be something
   that you want me to do
   that *is* exciting.

Help me,
   make me do it, Lord.

Amen.

Alone

Do

Next time you're feeling really rubbish and alone, try for once not to blame God for it all. It's easy to do it, but this time try instead to just sit and think about the wider picture, about the whole of your life. Perhaps this is just a blip in what's going on, a low point in a life that'll have millions of high points. Now thank God for the high points of your life and ask him to be with you as you try to survive what's going on now.

Think

Get a huge piece of paper and a thick felt-tip pen. Now write down in any way you want to all the things in your life that get you through each day. Think of people and places and memories and jokes and activities. Think of what you're looking forward to, what you dream about, what you wish for. Now pin this to the back of your door. Why? Simple. Read it every time you leave your room, no matter how you're feeling. Reinforce your brain with what's good about your life – it's important. Everyone needs to recharge.

Pray

I'm alone!
I'm alone!
Lord . . . you there?

I'm having trouble hearing you;
    maybe I'm not tuned in properly . . . just a minute.

No, still no good.

What is it then?
I pray,
   I go to church,
   I read the Bible (I do! I'm not lying!)
   and I chat to you all the time.

So what's wrong?
Why is it that when I need you the most
   you seem the most distant?

If only, just once,
   I could be a bit like Elijah
   and stand up
   against all the odds
   and my inhibitions.

But I can't.

I simply trust
   and hold on,
   even in the dark.
In the hope that in this darkness
   I will find both you
   and others who know you.

Amen.

Thinking about the future

Do

It's easy to let life take over. To fill your mind with questions or worries that probably aren't all that important. But what about those things that are important? The things that occasionally push into your mind and make you stop? Find out about a local charity, for the homeless, for old people, anything. See if you can spare any time in your busy life to help out. Remember, getting involved is exactly that. It's not swapping one life for another.

Think

You're busy, aren't you? Loads on your mind, stackloads to do and think about and decide. Sometimes it gets you down, the pressure builds, you want to jack it all in. Now think what it would be like if you weren't in a position to make any of these decisions. Just how lucky are you?

Pray

I'm confused, Lord.
(Again?) Yes, again!

At my age you have to think about the future;
   it no longer consists of toys,
   friends and sand-pits.

I need to know what I want to do.
I need to know why I'm here.

And I don't, Lord.
I have no idea at all.

I see so many who do.
They have aims, objectives.

Actually, they have one aim;
    to earn loads of cash for themselves,
    and to be rich, even if the job is boring
    (please don't let me be a solicitor, Lord).

I'd like that,
    but it isn't that simple, is it?
Not now I know you,
    because I have different things on my mind,
    like why is it that people are homeless
    and alone?

Things like that bother me, Lord,
    and I can't just sit here
    and think about me;
    I *want* and *need* to think about them, too.

Help me, Lord, to help them.

Amen.

Where am I going?

Do

Find everything you need to get through a normal day of your life. It doesn't matter what it is, if you think you need it, find it and put it on your bed. When you've finished, look at the pile of stuff you've collected and have a think – how much of this is really essential? If you think you can actually live without it, put it back where you got it from. Do this until you're down to the very basics for a day in your life. Not much left, is there?

Think

So, what do you really need to get through your life? What's really important? What helps you get through from one day to the next? What and who are part of your life's survival kit?

Pray

Right, God, that's it; I've had enough!
I've no purpose, no direction,
   and no clean pants!

I know that the last of these is trivial,
   but it acted as a catalyst to this whole situation.

WHERE AM I GOING?
Why won't you give me
   even a hint?

Nothing is becoming wonderfully clear,
    and I'm certainly not taking every step in song.
Every step seems to be taken in fear,
    through darkness and fog.

What *is* going on?
Do you *really* know?
Do you *really* care?

It's like being on a treasure hunt
    in the dark without a map
    or any knowledge about what the treasure is.

It's an adventure all right,
    but aren't you supposed to be a little bit prepared?
You know, rucksack, first aid kit,
    MAP!

Lord, I just need a little reassurance.
You make me mad, but at the same time,
    you hold me close.
Keep doing both, Lord.

Amen.

Old bones

Do

Start writing down all those times in your life when you're feeling so awful you just want to fade away but something happens which changes everything and suddenly you're on top of the world. Every time you experience something like this, write it down. Now, when you're feeling rubbish and as though everything may as well just end, read about what's been happening in your life and be amazed.

Think

Read Ezekiel 37:1-14. Read it again. Quite a story, isn't it? What do you reckon's going on here? Ever get the impression that your life is nothing more than a modern day equivalent of a valley of dead bones? Nothing left, everything's dead, everything's hopeless? What do you do when it seems all hope is lost?

Pray

Impressive, God,
    very impressive.
If you made me watch that
    I reckon I'd never question you again.
I might even think that the church has a future.

I know,
    I'm being bolshie,
    but I'm allowed
    because I'm me.

It's just that it seems to me
that we have a beautiful jigsaw to put together
but we just don't seem
to be able to put the pieces
in the right place.

We've got a few bits of sky
(they're the really difficult bits,
because they all look the same),
some green, landy bits,
and what looks to be some people,
but we just don't know where it all goes.

A bit like ourselves, really.
We can't sort out who or what we are,
so how can we manage to sort the world out?

I know, I know,
with your help.

I just needed reassuring, Lord,
that's all.

Amen.

How far would you go?

Do

Get on the Internet or get to a library. Do some research on people who've died for what they believed. People who've been put through hell because they stood up to be counted. People who changed the way the world thinks, the way the world lives. People who died so that the world would get the message.

Think

How do you cope when people question you about what you believe? How do you feel when people laugh at you and make fun of you? How do you react? What do you do? What's the right thing to do? Is there a right thing to do?

Pray

Standing by your beliefs
    is all very well, Lord.
You don't have to be a Christian to do it.
It's just something that most people do
    at some point
    in their lives.

But *dying* for them?
And not just dying, but horribly,
    and painfully.

I'm frightened, Lord.

You frighten me.

You expect us to follow you
    to the end.
To trust you,
    even to our deaths.

Would I have the courage, Lord?
Is my belief in you
    strong enough?

Why am I even asking these questions,
    when it is the answer
    that frightens me
    as much as the thought
    of dying for believing?

I have no way of ending this prayer.
As it is, I end it knowing that I hope against hope
    that I never have to make that choice.

Amen.

Temptation

Do

What's your weakness? What is it in your life that, when tempted, you really do give in to? It can be anything, no matter how small. So here's the challenge – concentrate on this one particular weakness, and deal with it. Instead of just giving in every time, focus on it, take control of it and do something about it. OK, so you'll fail now and again, but if you don't try, what's the point?

Think

It's not necessarily what's tempting you that's the issue, but your ability to take control of who and what you are. If you can't control something small, a tiny bit of temptation, how will you cope as life gets tougher and you face harder decisions, more temptations . . .

Pray

It's an odd thought, Lord,
   but in a way
   it's nice to know
   that you've been tempted too.

It means you understand
   a little more.
Not that you didn't before,
   but it makes me feel really at ease.

There's no way I can turn around
    and say,
    'You don't understand!
    You've never been there!'

You do,
    and you have.

So, Lord,
    that temptation
    and the way you said 'no',
    means more than simply
    you saying what you said
    and resisting.

It tells us
    that you don't just care;
    you know,
    and you understand
    all we go through
    and all we face.

Thanks, Lord.

Amen.

Punishment

Do

Amnesty International - you've heard about it, read a bit about it, now it's time to actually do something about it. So do some research, bother to find out exactly what Amnesty International is all about, get some of their leaflets, read up on what they do, what they think, what their aims are.

Think

Ever been punished? How did it feel? Ever punished someone else? Punishment isn't just a physical act, it's mental, social, political.

Pray

Punishment, Lord.
Making someone pay
    for what they've done.
It seems a sound enough policy.
They deserve it, for sure.
Some of the horrible things people do,
    locking them away from society
    is often the only answer.

So why, in this day and age,
    are our prisons overflowing?
It doesn't make sense.
We're supposed to be advanced as a civilisation
    but we're not, are we?

We inflict punishment
    and perhaps at the same time punish ourselves,
    as again we see another member of our society
    fall and falter and get locked away.

But what is the answer?
Education? *Execution*?

I don't know, Lord,
    but I've seen a glimpse of the answer:
    'Doctors don't do house calls
    for people who are fit.'

Perhaps our problem is that we're too wrapped up
    in the people who are fine,
    so that we don't care for those who aren't.

Help us nurse the wounded, Lord.

Amen.

Little things in life

Do

Is there something you love doing, something that doesn't take much effort or money, but that you haven't done for ages? Something that's been pushed out of your life by everything else, something that, when you think about it, you miss? What's stopping you doing it? Exactly – do it again. Now.

Think

Sometimes the big things in life take over. We let our lives become focused on big important bits and leave behind the smaller not-so-important bits. Think of it as a really good recipe – it's often the little bits that make all the difference, the salt and pepper and herbs. How are you going to add some extra seasoning to your life and give it a better taste?

Pray

Big things everywhere!
I can't move for them, Lord!
Exams, pressures,
    grades, assessments,
    relationships, parents . . .
    the list is endless.

I miss the times when little things
    were all that filled my mind.

When I was young
and I'd get fascinated
by bugs on flowers.

When catching minnows
in the little beck
was all I wanted to do
on a sunny day.

When sitting watching cartoons
in front of a roaring fire
was all that mattered.

Now there are big things.
Big, massive
scary things.
And they cast shadows everywhere, Lord,
obscuring my view
so that the little things
get hidden.

Be my torch, Lord,
and help me to discover
the little things again.

Amen.

Turning tables

Do

Read Matthew 21:12-14. Read it again. Now put yourself in that temple. Try to imagine the smells, the noise. Remember, this is a temple, a place where people go to worship. Now think about walking into your own church or any church and experiencing something similar – money changers, food stalls . . . How angry would you be?

Think

Now think about your own temple, your body. Are there things you do that aren't too great for your body? Things that affect the way you live, the way you think? What tables in your life need turning over?

Pray

Reading this bit, Lord,
   makes you think.
Throwing a few tables over
   and shouting a bit
    wasn't all it was about, was it?

Are we abusing your temple, Lord?

There's the temple of the church,
   and that seems all right.
Many have Christian bookshops

and coffee shops in them,
and they don't seem to detract
from the beauty of the place.

But what are they doing?
Preserving the building,
   or bringing people to you?
Pandering to tourists,
   or helping the needy?

What are *we* doing, Lord?
Do we, in our ignorance
   shut so many out,
   by our rituals,
   and arguments
   and differences?
Are we really doing
   what you called us to do?

Lord,
   knock the tables over
   in *all* of our temples.

Amen.

Nice shirt

Do

Look at what you wear when you go to church. Why do you dress the way you do? Think about what other people wear when they go to church. Who, exactly, are you all trying to impress? Why not dress down for a change? Why not go to church to meet God rather than show him your new trainers?

Think

How would you react if, when you were sitting in church, someone came in off the street and sat next to you? Now I'm not talking about your average Joe, but someone who's been on the street for weeks, months, years. Someone who can't remember the last time they washed. What would you do? Now imagine if that person coming in off the street was you . . .

Pray

I sat in church, Lord,
    all neat and tidy, in my best clothes.
Looking around, I could see that everyone else
    had pretty much done the same.
We all looked very neat, and tidy,
    and terribly middle-class.

You know,
    no *major* worries financially,

a decent house,
and no doubt a good holiday later on.

Then I thought,
'Imagine coming into church
off the street. How would I feel then?'

I don't even need to write a list,
do I, Lord?
You know that list as well as I.
A list that isn't written
but exists in the minds of so many.

How can we sort this one out, Lord?
You didn't ask us to become all comfortable,
and well dressed
and unapproachable.

You called us to go out and to welcome people to you.

Show us how to take off
these nicely pressed jackets,
roll up our sleeves and kneel down in the dirt
with those you came for.

Amen.

Nice shoes

Do

Ever found yourself saving up for something that you don't really need? A pair of trainers that cost a fortune, that aren't necessary, but will make you look really cool for about two weeks? Here's a challenge – every time you put in a pound towards whatever it is you're saving for, put just ten pence in another pot. Do this for every pound you save. Now, when you go to buy whatever it is you've been saving for, you've got some extra money to do something 'real' with. Choose a charity and give it away. Why not do this for everything you're saving for and, at the end of the year, add it all up and see just how much you're able to give? And I bet you'll hardly notice you're doing it.

Think

The people you know and love – are they with you because of how you look or because of how you are? Learn from the answer.

Pray

Just look at my wardrobe, Lord.
Full of clothes that are about as fashionable
    as my parents.
And I'm going out tonight.

How can I wear *any* of this?
What will my friends say?

They'll all be there in their new stuff
    while I sit around in these old rags.

It's not fair; how am I supposed to impress *anyone*
    looking so unfashionable?
They'll laugh, Lord, and make fun of me.

I know I shouldn't let it bother me, Lord.
That it's what's on the inside that matters.
It's just that sometimes
    it's nice to decorate what's inside
    with something on the outside,
    so that people don't have to look so hard
    to know I'm all right.

And I am all right, aren't I?
Sometimes I don't think so,
    which is why I'm so upset about my clothes.
I'm afraid of what people will think
    so I try to hide and be someone I'm not,
    when it's not the colours of my clothes
    I should worry about,
    but the colours of who and what I am.

Help me show them, Lord:
    my *true* colours.

Amen.

Willing to learn

Do

Read Mark 7:24-30. It's not the easiest of passages to get a hold of really. Jesus sounds like he's being pretty rude. But then he pretty much turns 180 degrees, as though he's perhaps realised something and changed his mind and is willing to learn from it. See if you can find a lesson more important than what we learn here. Difficult, isn't it?

Think

If Jesus was perfect, does that mean he didn't make mistakes? Or does it mean that he made mistakes and learned from them and grew and became even more amazing and perfect? Are you perfectly willing to learn?

Pray

Did you make mistakes, Lord?
I've read this story before
   and never thought about it like that.

I admit that I've never liked the idea
   of you never making a mistake,
   doing something wrong,
   or perhaps simply breaking
   one of your mum's vases.

If you didn't make *any* mistakes,
   then how could you have been God made human?
After all, all we ever seem to do
   is make mistakes!
Just look at me!

So, if you *did* make mistakes,
   you know what it's like to know you've messed up,
   or done something wrong,
   or upset someone.

You know how we feel.
You understand what we go through,
   but . . .

   you show us a way out.

A way to deal with it;
   a way to be perfect
   by admitting we were wrong
   and saying sorry.

Now that is what I call
   perfection.

Amen.

In with the animals

Do

If you can, visit a farm. If you can't, visit a zoo or something. Either way, get down to somewhere where animals live. Breathe in the smell, check out where they sleep. Now imagine what it was like in a cold stable. The muck, the smell, the sweat, the breath. And Jesus was born in this. What does this tell you about God? What does this tell you about the possibilities for your own life?

Think

God likes to do things differently. Mind you, how easily would you relate to a saviour born into a wealthy family? Someone who had it easy, didn't mix with the riff raff? Someone who would try to help people but wouldn't be able to see it from their point of view? Someone who had never actually been there, alongside them, in the muck and grime of their lives, trying to help?

Pray

'Where are you, Lord, and where am I?'
(I shouted that, so please take notice.)

You see, I look at my life
    and I am a little confused.
If there is a direction
    and I'm supposed to be following a pathway,
    then I don't seem to be able to stay on it.

I've wandered all over the place,
    doing this, doing that.
And here I am,
    still trying to find a signpost.
Nothing I've done seems to make sense
    or have a goal.

But if you take a look at the crib scene
    it hardly looks well planned either.
Well, it certainly wouldn't have done
    if I'd been there.

'In a *stable*? Baby in a *manger*?
Visits by *shepherds* and *forinuz*!
Lord, what *is* going on?'

Yep, I can hear myself now.
But it all makes sense when you look back.
It seems to fit.

Perhaps my life is like that too.
Is it clearer from where you are, Lord?

Can I have a look, sometime?

Amen.

Neighbours

Do

Is there someone you don't like? Is there someone you don't like because everyone else says you shouldn't like them because of the way they look, dress, speak, smell, live? Have you ever bothered to find out for yourself? What's stopping you? Scared?

Think

Have you ever been that person everyone else decides not to like? Perhaps you moved somewhere new and got pushed around a bit. Maybe it's because of something you do, something your family does. Maybe it's just because you go to church. How does it make you feel? Why do you think people are like this? Why do you think you're sometimes like this to others?

Pray

I have an idea, Lord.
What say I get dressed up
   and go to another church
   that doesn't know me?

Easy?
Well, let's say that in 'dressing up'
   I put on clothes that I rubbed in dirt
   (use your imagination)
   pour a rather large amount of cheap alcohol over me,

get my hair really greasy,
don't brush my teeth,
and *then* go to another church.

Now, that would be interesting!

You see,
   I know I wouldn't be welcomed.
That may be a harsh assumption
   and perhaps there *are* churches out there
   that would welcome someone like that;
   I just know that it is not the majority.

And it's sad.

After all,
   you weren't exactly the tidiest,
   neatest, cleanest customer,
   were you?

And if we reject people like that,
   how can we ever believe
   that we welcome you?

Amen.

Real wealth

Do

Think of everything you own, everything you have. Add up how much it's all worth, throwing in whatever cash you've got lying about on the floor, in your wallet, in the bank. Is this wealth? What makes you really wealthy? What are the things in your life that make you really rich? Write your real wealth on a small card and keep it in your wallet. Read it sometimes and smile.

Think

It's easy to get sidetracked. It's easy to follow the crowd and be convinced that because everyone else thinks it, it must be right. That money really is the be all and end all of what it's all about. OK, so it's important, but does your happiness truly depend on how much of it you have? Money can help us be happy, but does it necessarily make us happy?

Pray

Lord,
    I want to be rich,
    do well, be successful,
    and that's it.
    Sort of.

Some of my friends are like that:
    careers, money, cars,

houses, holidays.
Sounds great.

Sounds great, and average
    and dull and unexciting,
    and very un-me.

Yes, I'd like those things.
Money would no doubt help
    pay for the exciting things I want to do.
But surely my life is more than that.

Looking at where I am now,
    I can't really see
    how money would make much difference.
Clear my debts and that's it.
I don't *need* anything else.

What I do need
    is what I've already got:
    family, friends, support.

That's wealth to me.

Lord, am I rich?

Amen.

Make a difference

Do

Look at your life right now – is there anything about it that in some small way is making a difference, making people sit up and think, changing the world? Can you think and do anything that will cause perhaps just a little ripple? If you're thinking of excuses just think how short your life really is. Do you want it to count for something or count for nothing? What you gonna do?

Think

Excuses – we all use them. Any reason to not do something and we'll think of it. Just let the days drift on by because there's not enough time to do anything . . . Exactly! There's not enough time to do any-thing – there's enough time to do *something*! If there are excuses in your life stopping you from getting involved and making a differ-ence, work out what's more important, the excuse or what you want your life to say to the world.

Pray

There is one thing that frightens me, Lord:
    fading into obscurity.
Disappearing into nothingness,
    and simply being just another cog
    in the machine that is the general public.

I'm not asking for fame or fortune
    (but if that is a part of my future then

I'm sure I'll be fine!) –
simply to make a difference.

So many people I know
    are happy just to live their life
    in a way that keeps them fine
    and comfortable,
    and makes sure that their water is hot,
    their double glazing clean
    and their holidays abroad trouble-free.

I'm not.

I don't want to be just another statistic.
I want and *need* to make a difference:
    to the people I know and don't know,
    to this world and to what is happening in it.
I want to have an impact!

Is that too much to ask, Lord?
If it is,
    it doesn't really matter
    because I'm asking it anyway.

Lord, help me
    make a difference.

Amen.

I want

Do

Get a catalogue or a magzine and cut out all the things from it that either are or represent what you want. Stick them all to a dart board and thow darts at them. Every time you get one of the pictures, take it down, decide whether you really do need it or not. If you need it, put it in a bag, if you don't, throw it away. Do this until you have nothing on the dart board and are holding an empty bag. Now, what do you really, really want?

Think

Ever wondered what God wants you to want? Think about it. See if any of it has a designer label, a faster processor, better sound quality . . .

Pray

Does my praying annoy you, Lord?
Do I sound
   like a pestering little child
   in a supermarket
   who wants the toy on the top shelf
   and won't shut up
   until he gets it?

I sometimes wonder.

I don't mean to be,
   and I certainly don't want to be.
I don't want to ask or demand for things.

I simply want to learn to trust you.
That's not too much to ask, is it?
The trouble is
   I know that I can ask for things
   that I don't need
   and that I can whinge on at you
   and not do anything about it myself.

Not very clever, really.

I suppose what I should do a little more
   is not say,
   'I want...'
   but ask,
   'What do *you* want...'

Would that make more sense, Lord?

Is that what you want?

Amen.

Someone annoying you?

Do

There's someone you know who gets on your nerves. Someone who drives you up the wall, makes you want to scream and shout and . . . God loves that person. We're told to love our neighbours as we love ourselves. OK, so it's difficult, but can you meet the challenge, go to that person and do everything you can to love them? After all, 'love' doesn't necessarily involve 'like' . . .

Think

How difficult is it to really love people? To look beyond the bits you don't like, and still love them? How about the people you don't like, or those who don't like you?

Pray

There's someone in our church, Lord,
 and they're annoying me.
I know that's not really a surprise,
 but this one is really getting on my nerves.

I have an overwhelming urge
 to get extremely un-Christian with him
 and then be very un-Christian
 with my boot.

Did you ever feel like this?

Actually, Lord,
    do you ever feel like this *now*?

You see, the problem is
    that he's one of those 'perfect' Christians
    who is all smiles, prayers and Bible quotes.

That's fine,
    but he also thinks he runs the place
    and that he is right,
    and that his way
    is the only way.

And he says really annoying things, like,
    'The Lord has blessed me to say this . . .'
    or, 'The Lord is telling us to do this . . .'
It infuriates me!
I imagine you sitting up there saying,
    'I didn't! You've just not listened properly!'
He must make you mad too, but you still love him,
    and speak to him, and help him.

Now there's a thought, Lord . . .

Amen.

Power vs. purpose

Do

Write down all the things you really want out of life, no matter what they are. Look at the list – how much of it is to do with just getting stuff you want, earning lots, having great stuff? And how much of it is to do with making your life worthwhile? Write another list of what you want your life to mean. Finished? OK . . . how are you going to achieve the things on that list?

Think

What is the world telling you is important in your life? Are you beginning to believe it? Is it hard to keep sight of what's really important? How do you get the balance right? What's the Bible got to say about it? Have you spoken with anyone about what you really want your life to be about, or are you just going along with what everyone thinks you should be thinking?

Pray

Life's weird, Lord.
Everyone is obsessed with power,
    ambition, wealth.
These have all become
    very important.

And the reason it's all very weird
    is that they're not really that important
    to me.

Well, they are,
>
>but I wouldn't class them as a point of reference
>to the way I live my life.

Yes, I'd like to be in a responsible position,
>
>doing well
>and earning lots,
>but I'd rather make sure
>I'm doing something I enjoy,
>and which is worth doing.

Does that make sense?
I live in a world where everyone wants the power-trip,
>
>and it's difficult not to become the same.

Weighing it all up,
>
>I get so confused (again)
>and end up not knowing what to do.

It drives me nuts.

I don't want power, Lord . . .

. . . I want purpose.

Amen.

Sin

Do

This week you will have no doubt been annoyed or appalled at what someone was doing, what they've done, how they live. You'll have made a judgement about them, probably been quite annoyed, then rolled over and gone to sleep. Now think about what you do that isn't so great. What if everyone knew about all the rotten things you do and think? What if they all decided to do something about it? Next time you find yourself judging someone because of what they've done or are doing, think about what you do and reassess how you deal with the situation.

Think

It's easy to judge, easy to condemn. It's easy to see some sins as worse than others, to jump on the bandwagon and just join in the crowd of condemnation. But no sin is worse than any other, no matter what we think. The outcomes may be different, but sin is sin. Doing something wrong is doing something wrong, no matter how you dress it up. Odd thing is, though, we keep sinning, God keeps loving. Get the message?

Pray

The cold shower didn't work, Lord.
Don't know why I even thought it would.
Daft idea from a God with a sense of humour.
All I am is wet, cold

and in need of a dressing gown.
Cheers.

Is it meant to be this difficult, Lord?
You see, I'd be lying if I said
    I didn't want to do it,
    and that I never think about it; because I do.

Is it a sin?
Doesn't seem fair if it is,
    because I try and stop myself but can't.
I'll be doing anything, from snoozing
    to walking, and 'pop': in that thought goes.

But then so do lots of other thoughts,
    ones I'm really not proud of.
And as for the things I do and have done . . .
'Hi, and welcome to Sin World!'

Selfishness, greed, pride, judging . . .
    and there's more where that came from.
And they're all equally bad.
So, Lord,
    help me to deal with them like that,
    rather than let the occasional one slip
    or chastise myself because
    I'm weaker in one area than another.
Sin is sin, and you still love me.
Thanks, Lord.

Amen.

Jesus' death

Do

Read John 18:28-19:30. Now, if you can, just try to imagine the scene. This was a place dedicated to the painful death of people society had got annoyed with and wanted to dispose of as unpleasantly as possible. This was a place where criminals were attached by nails to trees and then dragged into the air to die in full view of anyone who cared to watch. Now think about hearing Jesus on that cross, as he says simply, 'Father, forgive them . . .'

Think

Jesus lived his life mixing with people that the religous types, the wealthy, either ignored or tried to eradicate. And in death he did the same, hanging by nails driven through his wrists and feet, between two thieves. He experienced a death so hideous it's impossible to believe it's ever happened to anyone. But it did. To people like you and me. To a man who told us to love one another as we love ourselves. A man who died and . . .

Pray

You won, Lord. You did it.
No army, no fighting,
    no glorious, flag-waving, crowd-pulling,
    televised extravaganza; but you won.

You turned the world and its methods

on its head by one simple phrase:
'Father, forgive . . .'

Trouble is, Lord, I'm finding it difficult
to feel the benefits of the victory.
In a world where 'bad' violence is beaten with
'good' violence.
In a world where revenge has replaced justice,
the words simply fall to the ground
and sink to the bottom of a puddle
in a darkened alley
where another mugging takes place.

Where is the victory, Lord?
What was the point if two thousand years later
we still haven't got it right?

But then I hear you and the criminal
hanging by your side: 'Today, in paradise . . .'

Forgiveness:
uncompromising,
unjudging, unconditional.

There is the hope.
And in that hope there is the victory,
won on a piece of wood on a hill.

Amen.

Resurrection

Do

Are there things sitting in your memory that you keep there but don't actually need? Are some of these memories unhelpful, the kind that you can't get rid of but when you remember them, make you upset? How do you expect to move on in life if you can't leave behind the old and move on? If it helps, think of just one of these memories. Write it down, read it with God, then cut it up into small pieces and get rid of it. Out with the old, in with the new – resurrect your mind.

Think

Jesus died – it's a historical fact. Thing is, he upset the status quo by coming back . . . apparently. His friends were scared for their own lives following his death. They hid, denied him, kept out of sight. They probably wondered how long it would be before they, too, were strung up. The last thing they wanted to do was draw attention to themselves. After all, their leader was dead, killed by the powers that be. He'd gone, it was over, so why should they continue? Why risk your life for something that's just been crucified? If they felt like this, why then would they invent a story about Jesus turning up again? Why would they spread the word about his resurrection? Why would they die for this story, if they'd just made it up?

Pray

I'm beginning to understand, Lord.
(Don't get too excited though.)

The resurrection, Lord.
Is it about you offering us new life?
Not just after death,
    but now?

That seems to make sense.
But my behaviour doesn't;
    I have an urge to cling on
    to the past
    and get immersed in the old
    rather than the new.
Daft, eh?

Why do I do it?
What is there to keep a hold?
Well,
    comfort, security,
    a sense of belonging.
I feel at home in the old;
    the new seems to want me to
    leave it all behind,
    risk it
    and lean totally
    on faith.

That's scary, Lord.
But you never promised comfort,
    or security, did you?

Resurrect me, Lord.

Amen.

Out with the old

Do

Look at all your clothes. Now imagine that one day you arrive home to find that everything has been thrown out and replaced with new stuff. How would you feel?

Think

Ever been in that position where someone wants you to change something you're used to, comfortable with, and you're not that interested? Ever put someone else in that position? Or have you ever just thrown away the old to replace it completely, without any thought of the consequences?

Pray

Right, that's it; I've had it.
You can take all this bloomin' tradition
   and shove it!

I am sick and tired of people whingeing on about how
   'It didn't used to be done like that,'
   or 'We've always done it like this.'
Well, phooey to all of it!

How can we ever step forward
   if we continually sit in the past refusing to get up?
It doesn't make sense!

Sorry, Lord, I'm ranting again, but I'm mad.
I never knew a few songs, a drama,
    a couple of candles and the word 'meditation'
    could cause so much trouble.

It's not as if it's radical, or that we want to rip out the pews,
    but people really do get angry
    if something they are used to is threatened.

But we're all bad at it, aren't we?
We've all got our individual ways of doing things.
I think the trouble is that we are far too much
    'all or nothing'.
Either change everything, or leave it as it is.
Daft, aren't we?

Traditions are built on new ideas that last.
Perhaps, these traditions
    are the foundations of what is to come.
Help us build on them, Lord.

Amen.

Always right

Do

Is there something over which you've fallen out with someone? Something that you argued about because you were utterly convinced you were right and they were wrong? Now look at whatever it was you were arguing about and try to see it from their point of view. Now try to understand why they thought what they did, and you something else. There probably wasn't anything to fall out about, was there?

Think

To really learn we have to see things from other people's points of view. Otherwise we depend on conclusions drawn when not all the evidence is present. Why is this dangerous?

Pray

I'm wrong! I'm always wrong!
Everything I say, do, believe, say, eat, sleep
   is wrong!

Except for what I said earlier.
That *was* right; it had to be.
It made total sense,
   was backed up by evidence
   and I won the argument.
What more proof could you need?

Well, a lot actually.
The only reason I won
    was because I was better at arguing,
    even though half way through
    I realised they were right.

A little bit pointless that, really.
And stupid.
It's not about winning the argument
    or being *proved* wrong
    but finding out what is right,
    and you can only do that by discussing,
    not arguing.

And by discussing
    you can admit when your views are wrong
    and openly explore new ideas.

That's how to learn.
That's how to develop.

That's how to develop faith.

Amen.

No favourites

Do

Picture someone you just don't like. Someone you can't get on with. Challenge yourself to get to know this person properly. This person is loved by God in exactly the same way as you. Try to see what God sees. No one said this life would be easy . . .

Think

No matter who you are or what you do, God loves you. Equally. Think about it.

Pray

Are you sure about this, Lord?
   Having no favourites means
   having no best friends,
    no one you can *really* trust.
Are you positive that's what you mean?

I just can't comprehend it.
How can you love me
   as much as St Peter?
And how can you love a drugs dealer
   as much as me?

It doesn't compute!
Information overload!
BOOM!

OK, I'm getting carried away,
    but I think it demonstrates what I mean.
This 'unconditional love'
    is a difficult idea
    for us humans to grasp.
We find it pretty impossible
    to love all as we should.

We have favourites
    as well as those we don't like at all.

It's difficult, Lord.
How do you love us all,
    completely?

Thank you, Lord,
    for the things I don't understand.

Amen.

Angels

Do

Research all you can about angels. Go to a library, watch a few films, anything. Get into your mind the many ideas of what angels are like.

Think

It's not all wings and haloes. Think of people you've met in your life who've made a difference to who and what you are. People who've made you think, changed you in some way. Picture every single one of them. Be thankful that you met them.

Pray

Angels, Lord! Well really!
How can you expect me to believe in them?
All white and winged and haloed.
All a bit daft, if you ask me.

And them guarding us?
An angel protecting us?

Sorry, Lord, I don't like being this cynical,
    but that's the way today's society makes you.
See, cynical again!
Useless, aren't I?

Anyway, back to this angel business.
I guess my problem is

that I'm letting the romantic get confused with the reality;
the reality being what I *perceive* to be the truth.

And that is that angels are those with you.
There, simple!
I say this because I know so many
    who I would class as angels.
Not because they are perfect,
    or that they are the best Christians ever.
No.

It is because of who they are
    and what I have learned from them.
You don't need a list, Lord.
You know who they are.

Thanks, Lord,
    for your real angels.

Amen.

Competition

Do

Find a sport or activity you've never done before. Learn about it, take part in it. It doesn't matter how good or bad you are, so long as you're enjoying it.

Think

Ever felt like you're always coming in last? That no matter what you do everything goes wrong? Always picked last or doing badly or not doing as well as everyone else? Now think of those moments when everything goes right and you feel on top of the world. Without the lows would the highs in life seem as high?

Pray

Lord,
    I'm not much good when it comes to competition,
    especially at school.
I've lost every running race,
    failed a few exams
    and never been picked for a team.
My life seems to be one continuous last place.

I sound low, don't I, Lord?
Don't mean to be.
And at least I haven't hired any hitmen
    to take out those who keep beating me.

You see, I understand why there's competition,
    it's just that it doesn't sit well with me
    and who I am.
I even lose when I'm racing myself.
How sad is that?

Life seems to be one massive competition.
Everyone against everyone else,
    trying to do better,
    get better results,
    earn more money.
But the trouble with competition
    is that there are always those who keep winning,
    and those of us who keep losing.
It doesn't seem very fair.

I think you've caught me at a bad time, Lord.
I'm sorry.
I'd just like to know that perhaps, one day,
    I'll get to the finishing line
    and you'll be there waiting.

Amen.

A mess

Do

Draw two columns on a piece of paper. One side is your good points, the other your bad. Write until both columns are as full as they can be or until your hand starts to hurt. Read the lists. Now throw the piece of paper away.

Think

God sees the good in us and the bad but from it all sees the potential of what we can become. Remembering the list of all your bad points? How does it make you feel knowing that even though you may not think you're that great, God looks at you and wants to help you become the best you can possibly be?

Pray

So, Lord,
    you can do anything with anything
    no matter how messy it is?
Excellent!
Well, it makes me feel a little better, anyway.

I'm the human equivalent of a well-used compost heap –
    lots of rubbish and a bit smelly.
But you reckon you can see the good in me,
    and from all of this
    you can create something great.

From me?
How is that possible?
I'm a bad Christian.
I question everything.
I do most things wrong.
I'm stubborn.

Do you really mean it, Lord?
That from me,
   little manky me,
   something good will come?
I hope so.
I don't want to be a waste.

Use the compost of me, Lord,
   and grow something beautiful.

Amen.

Purpose

Do

Write your ambitions on a sheet of paper addressed to yourself.
When finished, place in an envelope, seal it and place it in a safe
place. Do not open it for ten years.

Think

What is God's purpose for you? What have you been chosen to do?
What do you want your life to mean?

Pray

So, Lord,
    why do you choose such unlikely people?
I'm not just talking about Abraham and Sarah.
What about the disciples?
Or Jonah?

Or me?

I'm weird, Lord,
    very strange;
    hardly 'disciple' material.
I'm picky, annoying, angry, sad, happy, low, fussy,
    desperate, lonely, unsure, unconvinced, critical, crazy
    and obsessed with shoes.
So why did you pick me?

And, while we're on the subject of being 'picked',
    what have I been picked for?
Why won't you tell me?
I'm floating along,
    getting through life,
    not knowing what to do,
    where to go.
And you say you've chosen me!
That you have a purpose for me!
How insane does that sound?
Very.

Just let me in on the plan at some point, OK?
Thanks.

Amen.

People like me

Do

Find out about people in history who've done amazing things for the world. Read about their lives and learn from them. Take notice of the fact that more often than not, they're just ordinary people who stood for something and did something about it.

Think

You have one life on this earth and with it you can do something so amazing you won't believe it until it's happening. It might be frightening, it might push you so much that at points you're so tired you just want to give up, but isn't that what life's about? At what point was life ever meant to be easy?

Pray

I read the Bible, Lord
   (I do! Honest!),
   and I get the sense that
   woven into all the stories
   is a tremendous amount of theatrics.
That's not me being rude, Lord.
I love it!
All those unlikely heroes
   plucked from obscurity;
   all those really bad baddies.
It's great!

And all that subversive stuff –
   lots of toppling of pillars,
   and upsetting people who think they're important.
So much hope and strength
   coming from people who seem to be so 'normal',
   so full of insecurities, questions, problems.

People like me . . .

And that makes me think, Lord.
You used these people,
   like Moses,
   and moved mountains,
   often in spite of them.

Could you do the same with me, Lord?

Amen.

Making a difference

Do

Think of something in the world that really annoys you. Something you think that there's simply no justification for. Now work out how you're going to get invovled and use your life to help make a difference.

Think

There are things in this world that simply shouldn't happen – we all know it. And at times the list seems to be so long that we feel helpless. But it's people like you who make the difference, who change what happens in the world and make their life count for something.

Pray

A lot of things annoy me, Lord,
   and I know you know that.
But I need to say it.
I'm not talking small things here either,
   like the usual list I bring
   of homework, relationships, spots,
   and scabby knees.
I'm talking 'biggies',
   like homelessness,
   war,
   famine,
   abuse,
   loneliness,

racism,
sexism,
bigotry,
ignorance,
discrimination,
bullying . . .

And that's just the tip of the iceberg, Lord.

Such a long list of pain
    for such a beautiful world.
It's so sad, Lord,
    so unnecessary.
And I feel so small
    when I think, 'How can I make a difference?'
Because I don't feel that I can.

Help me, Lord,
    to bring in the changes.

Amen.

Freedom

Do

What makes you feel trapped? What makes you feel like you need to escape? Go for a walk and think about these situations and try to realise just how free you really are.

Think

Some people live lives where freedom is dead. They work in sweat houses making trainers for multinationals. They live in shanty towns and exist under the poverty line. They're trapped in their homes afraid to leave. They're lost in their own minds, unable to escape. How free are you? What does real freedom mean? What does it involve?

Pray

I can't define it, Lord,
  this 'freedom' thing.
In some ways I see myself as really free,
  because I am.
I'm in a position to control my future,
  to make something of myself.
I've got friends, family,
  and a social life.
I can choose what I want to do,
  when I want to.
So I'm fairly free, I can't deny it.

But occasionally, Lord,
I get a twinge inside,
   like a sense of panic,
   and I want to escape
   from this world,
   from where I am,
   from who I am.
I feel trapped,
   suffocated,
   shut up.

Am I ungrateful?
After all, so many millions are so less free than I am.
I'm lucky,
   but that doesn't make it any easier.

I'm sorry, Lord.
I just find it sad
   that in this 'free' world,
   with so much choice,
   so many of us feel trapped.

Free us all.

Amen.

Life plans

Do

Quickly sketch out the plan you have in your head for your life for the next few years. Pin it on your wall. Amend the plan as your life develops, new things crop up, you change your mind.

Think

Sometimes everything goes according to plan. Other times everything falls flat on its face. How do you cope with both these situations? Where does God fit into it all?

Pray

Plans, Lord,
    I'm supposed to be making plans.
I'm supposed to think about what I want to do,
    know where I want to be
    and plan my whole life . . . now.

I can't.
I don't want to.
I won't.

You see,
    it seems mad that the now me should know
      what the future me will want, and be, and enjoy, and do.
The now me wants adventure, excitement, the unknown . . .

not this career-path + marriage + retirement.
(Whatever any of that actually is.)

Am I mad?
I guess so, but I can't decide,
    and I need to make certain people think that I can.
Does that make sense?

You've given me this life,
    this gift of such hugeness,
    and I don't want to sign it over
    to what everyone else thinks I should do with it.
It's not selfish, or unrealistic,
    it's just the way I am.

And you made me!

And I thank you for that, Lord.
Thank you that I want to do something with my life,
    to live it to the full,
    to squeeze every drop of adventure from it,
    and be able to say, 'Here you go, Lord. I did it.'

Amen.

Prejudice

Do

You might not want to admit it but I guarantee there are things in this world about which you have a few prejudices. Want a challenge? Well, do some research on them, learn about those things that perhaps you're just that bit too judgemental about. Now try and see it all from another point of view, someone else's situation.

Think

Ever been bullied? Ever bullied someone? How does it feel? Why do you think it happens? Odds on that it usually boils down to something stupid like the colour of someone's hair, them being new, what their parents do, where they're from. It's no different in the wider world, is it?

Pray

I've got friends who've had fun made of them
    because of the colour of their hair.
They were bullied for that.
I mean, how stupid can you get?

Obviously very stupid.

We humans are so quick to judge
    and even quicker to lash out
      at what we don't understand
      or don't want to understand.

We use a big word to hide behind:
    prejudice.
At least by using that
    we can pretend someone somewhere
    is doing something about it.

But what we should be bothered about,
    and I mean really bothered,
    is what we're doing about it,
    and how we're making a difference.

Because at the moment, Lord,
    we're not.
So help me to be one of the few.

Amen.

A surprising life

Do

Grab a Bible and read 1 Samuel 17. Read it again and make appropriate sound effects. Now close your eyes and try to put yourself right there in the thick of it, witnessing exactly what happened when David stood up to Goliath.

Think

David sorted out one giant, but what of the giants today? They may not be enormous blokes with swords threatening to slice us in half, but they're probably just as, if not more, dangerous. What you going to do – stand up and fight, or run away?

Pray

David.
What's all that about then?
You, Lord, once again,
   chose the least obvious
   to beat the opposition.
Brilliant and daring in one punch.

Now, Lord,
   I'm not saying I've got aspirations to be king
   or go out killing giants,
   but I wouldn't mind thinking that perhaps
   this seven-stone weakling
   could be used in a similar way.

I want my life to be surprising,
    to be different.
There are plenty of giants to be knocked down today anyway,
    and although they're not big hairy blokes
    with big swords
    they're frightening enough.

I know I can't battle single-handed
    against poverty, homelessness, hunger . . .
But perhaps with a few stones
    I can make a dent or two,
    knock them off balance?

Be my sling, Lord.

Amen.

Getting away with it

Do

Find that Bible again and read 2 Samuel 11. On a scale of 1 to 10, just how insane are David's actions?

Think

Ever done something bad and thought you'd got away with it? Be honest . . . And what of those things you did that still no one knows about? How do you feel about what you did?

Pray

You do pick them, Lord.
David was great
   and David wasn't.
Misused his power,
   messed everything up . . .
   and you chose him.

I don't suppose you ever regretted that, did you?
I guess not.
You pretty much know what you're doing
   and seem able to make good
   out of a really lousy situation.

David was brilliant
   and bad.

He was a great leader
    and a weak man.
But you used him,
    despite of,
    and because of,
    his weaknesses.

Which makes David so much more approachable.
He's not perfect,
    he's not a shiny, haloed, glowing individual.
He's got more baggage than a bus load
    of retired tourists visiting Bournemouth.
He does good and bad.
And does both really rather well.

And if you can use someone like that
    you can use me.
Please?

Amen.

Forgiveness isn't an excuse

Do

Read 2 Samuel 12. Remember a time when you were found out for doing something you thought you'd got away with? How did you feel? What did you do?

Think

Ever done something deliberately wrong, thinking that it was OK because you'd be forgiven for it? Ever done something that wasn't perhaps too bad but was still wrong because you knew you could get away with it? Did you get away with it? How do you feel?

Pray

Well, Lord,
    when I say I'd like to be like David,
    I don't mean literally.
So you probably won't need
    a Nathan to come and tell me how bad I've been . . .
    I hope.

I know I do bad things,
    like anyone.
Some I mean to do,
    others I don't.
And sometimes I secretly think,
    'It's OK, God will forgive me.'

Which isn't very clever, is it?
(At least I've admitted it.)

I know you forgive,
   but that's not an excuse
   to do what I want,
   when I want,
   and then try to cover it up.
Or pretend it's OK
   because no one else knows.

But I do use it as an excuse,
   and I'm sorry.
I don't mean to be weak,
   but I am.

Build me, Lord,
   make me strong.

Amen.

Wisdom

Do

Find that bit in the Bible where Solomon threatens to cut a baby in half to sort out an argument between two women. (I'm not going to tell you where it is this time – do some detective work.) Read it. Now try to work out what Solomon was doing.

Think

Are there times when reading the Bible just confuses you? What do you do about it – give up or pray about it or ask for someone's help or just run away and pretend it didn't happen? What's the wisest course of action?

Pray

Solomon.
Wise?
Mad?
Both?
Mr Extreme Measures, methinks.
Don't think I'd be of the 'cutting a baby in half' brigade,
   but I see why he suggested it.

I'm trying to work out what this is telling me.
After all,
   people are always saying I should read the Bible,
   understand from it,
   learn from it.

Well, I'm not.
Not in this case, anyway.
What's swords and babies got to do
    with me and where I am?
Seems very strange
    and irrelevant.

Sorry if that's rude,
    but it's how I feel.
And if I'm to learn
    I've got to say when I'm not.

Help me understand, Lord,
    and give me patience when I don't.

Amen.

An obvious Christian

Do

Make a mental note of all the times today where people might think you're a Christian by what you do and what you say. Make sure to note all the times when they probably think the opposite.

Think

It's not easy being a Christian. But then it was never meant to be. Why do you find being a Christian difficult? What is it that you think you do wrong? What do you do right? What do you think God focuses on?

Pray

Lord,
   loads of Christians seem to be really obvious about it.
They talk about it,
   know the Bible back to front,
   have a prayer for everything,
   love you,
   tell everyone about the above four,
   and apparently don't sleep
   because they're too busy praying.

I'm not . . .
   obvious, that is, about being a Christian.
At least I don't think so.

I'm fairly scared of talking about it,
   I don't read the Bible much,
   I pray about a few things occasionally,
   and I think I love you.
What does that mean?
What does it say about me?
What does it say about them?
What does it say about you?
What am I on about?

But I believe in you, which is a start.
And I do pray.
And some other stuff.
Is that OK for starters?
If so, can we make the main course
   really really appetising?

Cheers, Lord.

Amen.

Little soon becomes big

Do

This is a don't . . . next time you see someone being picked on or hear rumours being spread, don't join in. Now you're not a part of it, how are you going to change it? Do something . . .

Think

It's easy – a rumour starts from nothing, spreads quickly and soon everyone believes something that probably isn't true or is so far from the truth it's hard to believe anyone could actually think it. It's like that in playgrounds – that's why people get bullied and picked on. But it's nothing more than a small version of what happens in the wider world between different groups of people in different countries and cultures. Something small soon becomes something big and then someone gets hurt or killed and then . . .

Pray

I'm not, Lord,
   prejudiced, that is.
At least I didn't think so;
   until today.

This kid in class,
   the weird skinny one with spots and smells
   (as in aromas that make your stomach churn)
   was being annoying.

Well, he was sat at the front
asking questions
and answering, too.
Just how spoddy is that?

So after lessons
some of the class made fun of him,
threw his bag on the roof
and we all laughed.

Not clever . . . or nice.
Just stupid
and prejudiced
against someone who was 'different'.
That's it.
And I'm sorry.
Because it's made me realise
that if it can happen in school
to someone with spots
who knows the answers,
what if it happens
in a country
to thousands who believe
or look different?

We're a stained society, Lord.
Wash us.

Amen.

Behind the scenes

Do

Read a chapter of a novel. Now think about what might be going on behind the scenes. What the characters are getting up to when they're not being written about. Where they go to relax, to live, to chill out, to laugh, to cry.

Think

Stories in the Bible need us to think that little bit further about what's going on. We get the bare bones of what's going on but if we just use our imagination, do a bit of research, we can get a real feel for what's going on. Think about what's happening behind the scenes.

Pray

The trouble with me, Lord,
    (What? There's only one?)
    is that when I read the Bible,
    I don't read it.
I don't look behind the scenes
    to try and imagine what else was going on.

Take the soldiers that carried out the slaughter:
    what happened to them?
Did some of them turn to you?
Now there's a thought;

someone sent to kill you
ends up following you –
kind of a full circle.

And then there are all the other characters:
    what about the soldiers who crucified you?
And the people at the wedding with the wine incident?
Or the 5000?

So much was going on
    and we miss it because we're blind to it
    and don't want to look any further.

But maybe,
    just maybe,
    it's by looking that little bit further
    that we start to learn.

Amen.

Being judgemental

Do

Think you know all the facts about something you've got strong views about? Guess again. Do some research and really find out about it.

Think

It's easy to judge. All you need is blinkers, a lot of the facts missing from your brain and a lack of care for others. And yet we still do it. Think about that for a moment.

Pray

Lord,
   what I find frightening
   isn't that other people can react
   and hurt others
   by being judgemental,
   but that *I* can.
And I do.
From small things at school
   to big things in the world.
And I don't even realise I'm doing it.
How awful is that?

I'm not happy about it.
It's not very 'you'.

I'm supposed to love my neighbour
   and follow you.
Bung those together
   and I've got to have unconditional love
   for everyone else.

That's frightening.
It's also exciting,
   and amazing.

Help me, Lord,
   to be unconditional
   in my love.

Amen.

Money in your pocket

Do

Every time you spend something and have only coppers left, save them. Put them in a pot in your room. Do this for 12 months. Count up what you've managed to save. Now give it all away.

Think

How often have you bought something you simply didn't need? How many times have you been persuaded by colourful adverts to empty your wallet and end up with something you can easily live without?

Pray

I can't believe it, Lord.
I've done it again.
A little bit of money in my pocket,
    then it's gone.
Well, it's still a little I guess:
    I've got three pence left from the tenner I had earlier.
And nothing to show for it.

Duped again.
Sucked in by sparkly shop windows,
    colourful colourfulness
    and adverts that work.
I'm almost ashamed.

So there I was,
    bag full of things I'd bought
    but didn't know why,
    leaving the shop,
    and I happened to pass someone
    asking for money.

They looked pretty homeless
    but I had nothing to give,
    except this three pence.
And I felt too guilty to only give that.
Not right, is it, Lord?

Next time,
    when I'm out
    and the adverts are whispering,
    help me to hear the whispers of others
    who need my money
    more than I needed this T-shirt.

Amen.

Unconditional love

Do

Love: what does it mean to you? Try to express it in any way you can by writing, painting, drawing, dancing, sitting, thinking, screaming, yelling, laughing, shouting, running . . .

Think

Unconditional – what do you think it really means? Look at Jesus' life, what he did, what he said, why he died . . . getting a better understanding?

Pray

Unconditional love is an amazing thing.
By its very nature it crosses over everything
 and still exists.
You can ignore it,
 insult it,
 do bad against it,
 try and kill it,
 but it's still there
 and it's still loving you;
 unconditionally.

So why do people (including me, Lord) find it so hard
 to understand?
Simple; they (we) want unconditional love
 with conditions.

We want to preach about it
  but not have to love someone who's gay.
We want to believe in it
  so long as we don't have to hug that bloke
  who committed murder.
We want to sell it
  as long as we are safe in the knowledge that some people
  will never, ever, get into heaven.

Not exactly unconditional.
Not exactly 'died on the cross' love.
But that's us, Lord, and some of us are trying to get it right.

Love us all, Lord,
  regardless of what we are,
  with your unconditional love.

Amen.

Death

Do

Find out about how other religions deal with death. Look at what they think it means, where it leads, how they celebrate life.

Think

Jesus was a real person, someone recorded in history. He existed, walked, lived, breathed, laughed. He had friends, family, followers. He died. Now this is where it gets difficult, because his friends saw him again after he'd been killed. He spoke to them, walked with them . . . Did they make this up or is it the truth? If it's the truth, if he did kick death in the teeth, where does this leave us?

Pray

Lord,
   this whole death thing . . .
   bit scary really.
I've been told I'm supposed to be 'unafraid'
   because I'm a Christian.
Well, stuff that.
Death frightens me – to death.

I don't want to die.
I don't want to experience the pain.
I imagine it all,
   I have nightmares about how I'll die!
It's not nice, Lord!

Sorry.
Very morbid, I know,
    but it's a difficult thing to get away from.

What was it like, Lord?
Dying?
Don't answer.

Oh, Lord,
    I don't know what this is about.
Just fear I guess;
    like the monsters under the bed.
All very real to me.
I hope you understand.

Amen.

Faith

Do

Read Mark 5:25-34. This is what faith's all about. Put yourself in that crowd as the woman is healed, as she gets better right there in front of you. What would you do?

Think

Apparently faith can move mountains. OK, so it's basically a metaphor, but if it can, if faith can be that powerful, what can your faith help you to do? What are you going to do about it?

Pray

That's faith, Lord;
    to know she could be healed just by touching your cloak.
Amazing.
I sometimes feel I have a faith like that.
But it's only sometimes, Lord.
Most of the time
    I question everything I do,
    everything I think,
    everything I believe.
There's nothing wrong with questions
    but they can take over.
And they do.

I forget what I'm about,
    what you're about.

I get swept up by the world,
   by its cynicism,
   by its obsessions.
I become like everyone else,
   when the whole point
   is that I'm not like everyone else.

And the crowd can be so crushing,
   sweeping me under,
   as I desperately try
   to keep my eye on you.

Help me reach out to you, Lord,
   and touch your cloak.

Amen.

Persecuted Prophets

Do

Got something burning a hole in your head? Is there something sitting rather uncomfortably in your mind and you need to do something about it? The question isn't whether or not you'll do something . . . but how far you'll go to get your message across. What are you going to do about it? Come on! Get off that sofa and do something. Now!

Think

Throughout history people have been persecuted for turning round to the world and shouting, 'Look! This is wrong! Why are you doing this?' It's a simple case of numbers: those in power are more than happy to silence the truth with a sword, a bullet, a bomb. But the trouble with the truth and the people who speak it is that it keeps coming back.

Pray

Prophets have a habit of getting killed, Lord.
Or at least having something horrible happen to them.

Even today,
    someone stands up,
    speaks the truth about injustice,
    and bingo:

a bullet to the brain –
or something.

But before you know it,
    someone else is there.
And another,
    and another.

And they're all slammed in prison.

The world seems to hate having the mirror
    thrust in its face.
The grime's obvious and ugly.
Best to smash the mirror
    or hide it and hope everyone forgets it was ever there.

But the grime won't budge
    and the reflection stays the same.
Be with them, Lord:
    your people persecuted.

Amen.

Extraordinary

Do

Ever thought of doing something different, something surprising, something extraordinary? What's stopping you doing it now? Nothing? Well get on with it then! Stop wasting time!

Think

Life can be one of two things: ordinary or extraordinary. It can either be something that just happens, continues, then ends. Or it can be something that surprises the world, makes people sit up and think, challenges them. The choice is yours.

Pray

Lord,
   I've been thinking . . .
   (dangerous I know).
It seems to me
   that the people you use
   are just ordinary everyday people
   like me.
Yet you choose them
   and use them
   and something amazing happens.

It strikes me as odd
   that sometimes you like the subtle approach
   and then opt for something really out of the ordinary.

Why is that?

I don't need an answer.

Why do I ask, though?
Well, I'm pretty ordinary
   and I wouldn't mind something theatrical and extraordinary
   happening to me.
Is that OK?
It's not a request or a demand;
   just a thought.

Thanks for listening.

Amen.

Virgin birth

Do

Read Luke 1:26-56. Think about how Mary may have felt when the angel came with its news. After all, she wasn't married and now she was going to have a baby. That's something very serious in a society that didn't look too kindly on women having children outside of marriage. Now think about trying to convince everyone that God was actually the father . . .

Think

Jesus was a living breathing son of three parents; God, Mary and Joseph. He experienced growing up, falling out with his Mum and Dad, helping them around the house. And yet he was also the son of God. It was a hands-on approach to getting involved with the world.

Pray

There you go again!
Theatrics,
   making an impression,
   doing things differently.
Mary must have been pretty shocked,
   and as for poor Joseph . . .

Wonder what that must have been like;
   to be the 'parents' of God's son.
A little bit of pressure, you'd think.

I often wonder how my parents feel.
I'm no 'God's son' that's for sure,
   but I guess I'm pretty special.
I'm here for a start,
   and that's quite something.
I can breathe,
   I can live,
   I can make a difference.

So perhaps,
   with a bit of divine intervention,
   something great
   can come from my humble beginnings?

Help me see outside the stable, Lord.

Amen.

No room

Do

Read Luke 2:1-7. Now do some exercise and get yourself really worn out. Now imagine being even more tired than that from miles and miles of travel, being pregnant and then being turned away from where you were expecting to stay. Now how tired do you feel?

Think

Biblical translations are funny things. Apparently the word we all assume means 'Inn' would be more accurately translated as 'guest room'. So here we've got Joseph and Mary not being allowed to stay in a guest room. This perhaps suggests that they were staying in a private house, perhaps even with relatives. So why didn't they let Mary and Joseph stay? What do you think?

Pray

Well, there's a turn up for the books.
All this time I've thought it was an inn
   and now perhaps I think it wasn't.
Turned away from the guest room . . .
   now that's plain rude.

But then, if Joseph was going to his 'home town',
   I never could quite understand
   why he tried to stay in a pub.
Surely he had family there?

Anyway, what it brings home
    is the world into which you were born;
    a world rejecting you from the beginning.
And you were only a baby!
They hadn't seen anything yet!
Then Herod gets all worked up
    and tries to kill you.
You attracted trouble, that's for sure.

But for what?
Turning the tables over, that's what.
The tables not just in the temple
    but in people's lives.
Their ideologies, their beliefs,
    their weaknesses,
    their misconceptions . . .
    all thrown onto the floor and scattered
    by you.

Amazing.
Help me turn a few tables over, Lord.

Amen.

Accepting Forgiveness

Do

Is there something you hide away inside, something you did that you said sorry for, were forgiven, but you still have it hanging round your neck making you feel a bit rubbish? Time to get rid of it by saying sorry one final time, accepting that you've been forgiven and then forgetting it and moving on.

Think

It's not the saying sorry that's often the problem, but the accepting that you've been forgiven, by yourself, by others, by God.

Pray

Temptation, Lord.
Oh dear, indeed.
Causes big problems.
Big scary ones that get in the way . . . of everything.

You seemed to be able to deal with it, though.
(Not really a surprise, I'll admit.)
And at least that tells me you do know what I'm going through.

But how did you do it?
How did you cope?
How come you never gave in?

I find it hard, Lord, almost impossible.
Some temptations just appear,
    others reappear – a lot.
And I don't like it.
And when I give in I feel dirty,
    even if I am forgiven.

You understand, don't you?
You know what I'm on about?
Like now, about that thing I did today?
I'm really sorry and I don't want to feel dirty.
Forgive me and wash away the grime.

Perhaps that's it, Lord;
    it's not necessarily temptation that's the problem.
It's the saying sorry and then accepting you're forgiven
    and then moving on that we find so hard.

Maybe that's why we keep falling down?

Amen.

Church

Do

Find yourself falling asleep during a service? Is church getting dull? Well what are you going to do about it? Not much by complaining. Get involved, get active, do something.

Think

Sometimes we forget that God doesn't live in church and that out in the real world, in every day of our lives, God exists. How often do you make the effort to see God in the world around you?

Pray

Lord,
    church can't half be dull.
I didn't used to go,
    and now I do,
    because I think I should.
That doesn't make it easier.

There are so many other things I'd rather do:
    like sleep in, walk the dog,
    or eat worms.

Sorry, that's not nice,
    but it's close to being true.
I'm told I can meet you there!

What? I meet you everywhere,
    and more often than not,
    when I'm *not* in church.

Like when I'm out shopping,
    or with friends,
    or just about to go to sleep.
You're everywhere, Lord,
    but church seems to be a bit of a barrier.

I'm not going to give up, Lord.
Going to church gives me a chance
    to meet others who chat to you; that's good.
And who knows,
    perhaps I'll be able to teach them something!

(Sorry to be cheeky, Lord.)

Amen.

Not the norm

Do

Read Luke 13:10-17, and see beyond the words. This wasn't a simple case of healing a bad back. Why didn't Jesus just say, 'You are healed', and instead go for, 'You're free from your illness'? What was he really getting at? Why did he throw in some liberation rather than simply taking away the pain?

Think

What things in your life keep you weighed down? After all, visible illness isn't always that which makes us unhealthy. Sometimes we need a bit of liberation ourselves, rather than a couple of pills to make us better or dull the pain.

Pray

It has to be said, Lord,
    you like to upset the norm.
I like that;
    it's exciting.
The norm?
Well, that's about as much fun
    as something that isn't.

OK, so it's only my opinion,
    but if the norm is wrong,
        then it really needs changing.

And that's what you did here, Lord.
In the most beautiful and gentle
    and powerful way.
No violence,
    no yelling,
    just a gentle, 'You can't be serious!'
And at a guess, that was followed by a little smile
    that said more than any speech.

Help me not to be normal, Lord.
I prefer the extremes.

Amen.

Jesus?

Do

Read Luke 23:49-24:12, 34. Put yourself in Mary's place. You've lost someone you loved more than life itself. Seen them ridiculed, tortured and then nailed to some wood and pulled into the sky to die a death of suffocation, exhaustion, dehydration and pure agony. Then one early morning, when you go to their tomb, you see someone familiar . . .

Think

What would you have said to Jesus if, after everything that had happened, you'd met him again, seen him, spoken to him? How would it change your life? How does it change it now?

Pray

I often wonder what it was like, Lord,
   to go to the garden
   and find an empty tomb.
Amazing.

Meeting those messengers
   must have been one of the most important meetings
   Mary ever had
   (short of actually meeting you, of course).

To be the first,
   the first to seek you

and hear the Good News
after all the hell of the weekend . . .

I'm in awe, Lord.
In awe of what Mary experienced,
    of what happened at that moment,
    and how it has affected the world since.

Mary was there, Lord.
That's important.
Perhaps we should all listen a little closer
    to people like her.

Amen.

You wore what to church?

Do

Find your scruffiest clothes and go to church in them. See if anyone notices or says anything. If they do, ask them what's more important, you being there or what you're wearing when you turn up?

Think

What differences are there between the churches? How many different ways of doing things exist in the ways we worship God? Does any of it actually matter? Who thinks it's important – us or God?

Pray

People say religion causes loads of problems.
(Oh, hi, Lord.)
They're right; it does.
Or is at least used as an excuse.

But what amazes me
    is how it's used against itself.
I mean, Lord, what's going on here?
Why do we care about labels?
Why can't we just move on
    and accept that we all differ?

And if it's OK to stick my neck out a bit,
    I bet you don't really care that much.

I bet you're not fussed how people get baptised,
   how they have communion,
   whether they're Roman Catholic or C of E,
   or if they dress nicely for morning worship.

None of that's important.
You said so.
You said so a lot.

Perhaps it's about time we started listening
   and instead of blaming,
   be slow to criticise others
   and quick to help them.

That makes much more sense.

Amen.

Real responsibility

Do

Think of the things you've done wrong today. Write them down and try to come up with a brief explanation as to why they happened and who was really responsible. In other words, don't make excuses and blame someone else.

Think

Why do you sin? Why do you do things you know you shouldn't do? Is it because you were born to sin and don't know any different? Or is it because you're human, with a freedom to choose which way to go, which path to follow? Isn't it all about taking responsibility?

Pray

Born into sin?
Lord, that sounds crazy.
I know there's an argument somewhere
   about something,
     (you can tell I really understand it)
   but it does sound mad.

Am I wrong? Out of order?
I dunno.
I just don't like the notion that we're born to it.
I guess humanity as a whole
   is responsible for some of the rubbish,
   but that's different from blame.

Compare me to a new-born;
   or a twenty-something
   to a four-year-old.
Seems to me that's pretty unfair.
Because if we're born to it,
   who's actually to blame?
No one by the sound of it.

We grow into sin
   because we're human and full of failures.
But you love us and help us.
Perhaps we should concentrate on that
   a bit more instead?

Amen.

S :00   1100 - 530
M 00
T 00
W 00
Th 00
Fri 00
Sat 00   900 - 600

hello.
morning.
wimbledon.
muscell speaking.
how can i help.